THE CBT JOURNAL
FOR MENTAL HEALTH

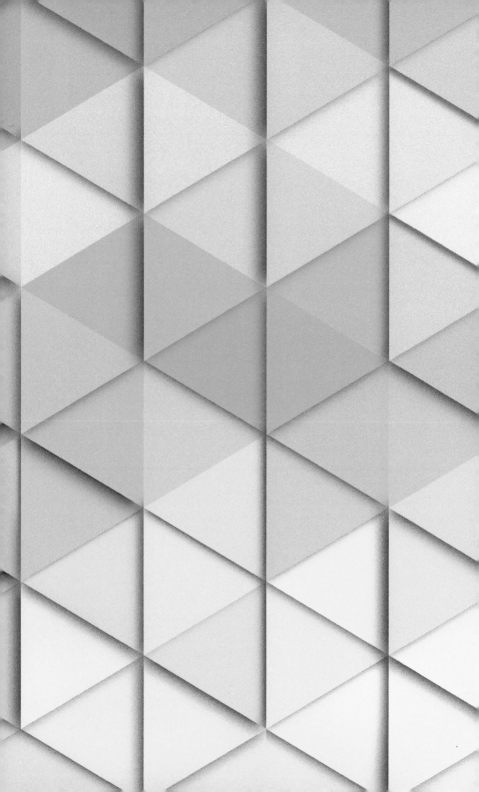

THE CBT **JOURNAL** FOR MENTAL HEALTH

Evidence-Based Prompts to
IMPROVE YOUR WELL-BEING

JORDAN A. MADISON, LCMFT

ROCKRIDGE
PRESS

Interior and Cover Designer: Alan Carr
Art Producer: Melissa Malinowsky
Editor: Alexis Sattler
Production Editor: Jael Fogle
Production Manager: Holly Haydash

All illustrations used under license from iStock

Paperback ISBN: 978-1-63878-882-9
R0

THIS JOURNAL BELONGS TO:

me Bitch!!

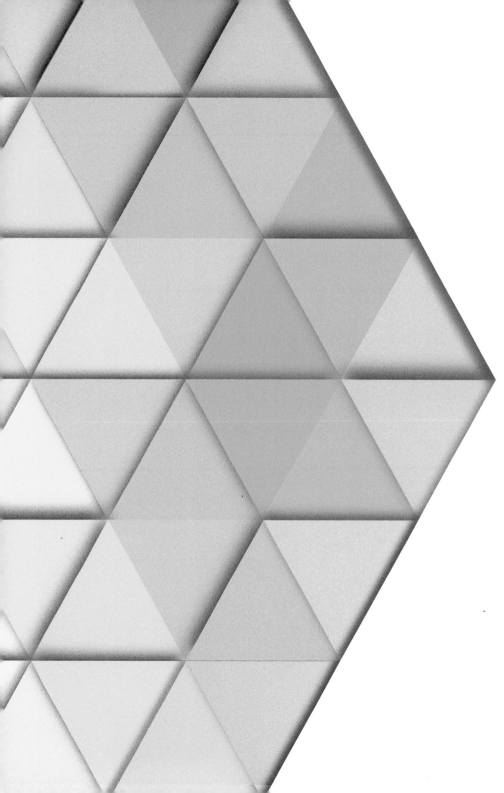

Contents

Introduction

Welcome to *The CBT Journal for Mental Health*. If you're reading this book, you may be looking for ways to improve your state of well-being. You are not alone. Everyone experiences barriers that block them from being where they would like to be emotionally, mentally, or even socially. While it's important to acknowledge that not all barriers are within your control, such as systemic oppression, poverty, or health challenges, my hope is that this journal allows you to identify those that are, explore where they are rooted, and begin to respond to them by reframing your thoughts, emotions, and behaviors. In becoming more mindful of your thoughts in this way, you may find that you feel more confident in yourself and that you behave in a way that sustains healthy relationships with yourself and others.

Before we get started, let me introduce myself. I am a licensed marriage and family therapist. I assist my clients with navigating their emotions, stressors, and relationships. I incorporate CBT techniques into most of my sessions and find that many of the problems we face boil down to how we think about them. Even as a therapist, I struggle with negative thought patterns and I question myself. I sometimes doubt if I'm doing enough for my clients or if I'm deserving of the success I've attained. But I find ways to replace my negative thinking with positive reminders, and by the end of this book, you will be able to as well.

Mental Health Basics

Because this journal is a jumping-off point to improving your mental health, it's important to cover some basics. The World Health Organization recognizes mental health as an essential component of our health. It not only encompasses our thoughts and emotions, but also how we handle stress and relate to the people around us. The three main components are our emotional, psychological, and social well-being, which all interact with each other. For instance, if you've been experiencing a lot of negative emotions (emotional well-being), it's likely you may not be able to focus on tasks (psychological well-being) or want to interact with others (social well-being).

Everyone has mental health, but not everyone has a mental illness. Mental illnesses are conditions that impair thoughts, feelings, and behaviors in a way that makes daily functioning difficult. This is why having positive mental health is so important. When your mental health is not its best, it is more likely to lead to mental illness. Some warning signs that your mental health could use improvement include persistent feelings of sadness, anxiousness, or hopelessness. Changes in eating and sleeping habits, isolating yourself from others, and difficulty concentrating are also signs that your mental health may be suffering. If you're noticing these changes, do your best to find healthy coping mechanisms that make you feel better.

One coping mechanism that I often use is journaling—probably what led me to writing this book. Journaling is beneficial to mental health because it allows you to process and release your emotions in a safe place.

It provides space to look at your progress and notice patterns in your moods and experiences as well. Nevertheless, this guided journal does not replace therapy, and it doesn't replace medication or medical treatment. So, if you are experiencing persistent negative feelings, thoughts, or behaviors, please reach out to a licensed mental health professional in your area, if accessible to you. You are far from alone, and there is nothing wrong with seeking help.

WHAT IS CBT?

Cognitive Behavioral Therapy (CBT) is a therapeutic technique that focuses on how cognitions, emotions, and behaviors influence each other. It was inspired by the work of Albert Ellis and Aaron Beck, who believed that the way to change behavior was first to change attitude. CBT focuses on identifying problematic behaviors and the negative thoughts that coincide with them, challenging them, and altering thought patterns and behaviors into healthier ones.

CBT is an evidence-based practice, meaning it has been research tested and proven to be effective. It is most commonly used to relieve symptoms of anxiety and depression. But it has also been shown to treat a wide range of other conditions, like addiction, anger, eating disorders, insomnia, phobias, low self-esteem, marital distress, and sexual dysfunction. One of the reasons CBT is so effective is that a CBT therapist acts as a coach, helping individuals learn to be their own therapist. It is also goal oriented and time sensitive, so clients are usually only seen for a certain number of sessions in order to accomplish a specific objective.

Some of the CBT interventions that make this approach so beneficial entail learning to recognize the distortions in your thinking that are creating problematic behavior, keeping thought and behavior logs, setting goals, using problem-solving skills to manage stressors, and implementing relaxation techniques. Homework and journaling are essential aspects of CBT because they allow for practice and growth in actual daily situations.

Keep in mind that thoughts, behaviors, and emotions are inextricably intertwined. This means that your beliefs can evoke emotions and behaviors as a response, and your emotions can also influence your thoughts and behaviors. Using CBT to reframe thoughts into more positive ones and thereby change behaviors to be more helpful can improve functioning, problem-solving, and interactions with others. In other words, it can improve mental health.

HOW TO USE THIS JOURNAL

The best way to use this journal is to take it one section at a time. Part 1 assesses your current mental health state. It gives you space to define goals, values, and areas that need improvement. Part 2 identifies the negative self-talk and thoughts you're holding, where they stem from, and how to reframe them. Part 3 addresses your behaviors and how they are affecting your relationships. Part 4 focuses on moving forward, managing your emotions, coping with stressors, and performing self-care. It is best to tackle the sections in order; they build upon one another.

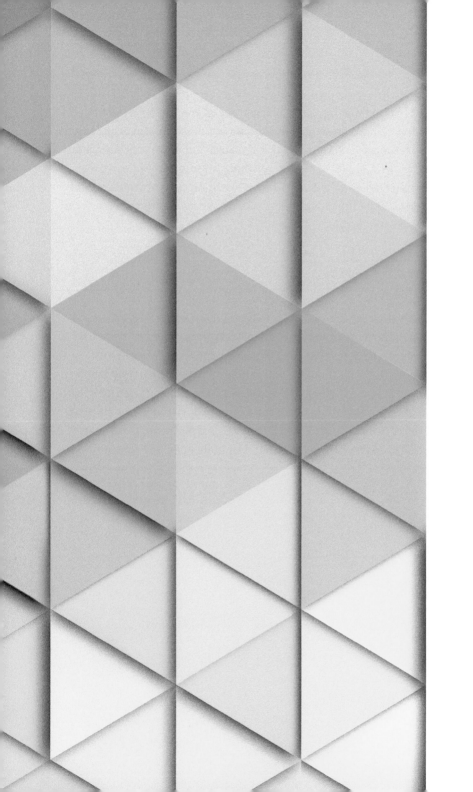

1

GETTING STARTED

The first stage of CBT is assessment. This section will help you evaluate your current state of well-being, mentally, emotionally, and socially. CBT works best when there is a clear definition of the problem. Once you are able to identify obstacles within your control that are holding you back from living the life you desire, you can then begin to focus on your mental health goals. Goals are typically a product of what you value. A key component to CBT is understanding your core values, because they have a direct impact on how you think. This section will help you explore what you value most, and if your behavior aligns with those values.

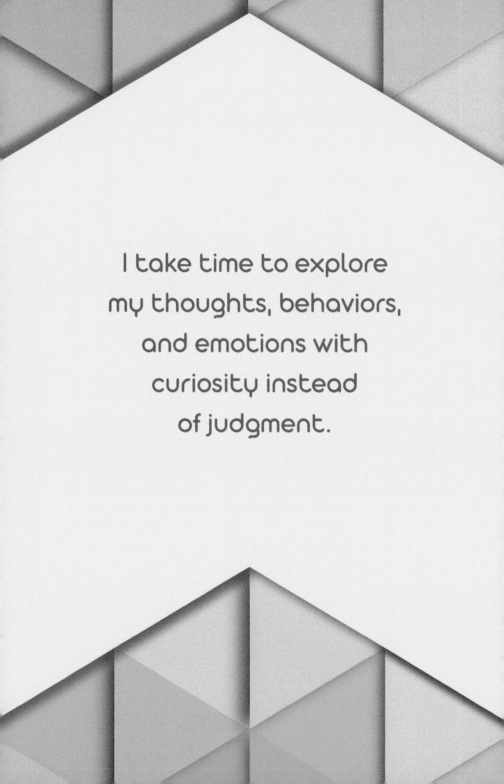

I take time to explore
my thoughts, behaviors,
and emotions with
curiosity instead
of judgment.

CHECK IN

How would you define the problems you are facing in your life right now? Could any problems be attributed to your internal beliefs or sense of self-regard? If so, what thoughts and behaviors have you noticed occurring frequently or not enough?

May 2022 - overweight - my clothes don't fit
- connecting with my family
- money
- Alcohol & Dylan's Alch use

GETTING GROUNDED IN
5 . . . 4 . . . 3 . . . 2 . . . 1

Grounding immediately connects you with the present moment. We often think about the future and all we need to do, making us anxious. Implementing grounding techniques daily can tamp down feelings of anxiety. If for any reason you are unable to do any of the steps, you can modify a step by taking five deep breaths, inhaling through your nose and exhaling through your mouth. Or you can give yourself a hug while you count to 10.

1. Notice **5** things that you can **see** right now.

2. Feel for **4** things that you can **touch** near you.

3. Listen for **3** things that you can **hear** at the moment.

4. Notice **2** things that you can **smell** around you.

5. Imagine or actually get **1** thing that you can **taste** right now.

By doing this exercise, you can use all of your senses to bring yourself back to the present. How do you feel after doing this practice? Was it useful?

Take a second to think about the past two weeks, and how you have been feeling. What emotions have been coming up for you? Write down instances that triggered negative emotions for you. Do you notice any themes when it comes to what triggers you?

Think about how you have been speaking to yourself and the words you've been using to describe yourself lately. Have you been speaking to yourself gently and with compassion? If not, what has your inner critic been saying to you? Is it your voice that you hear or someone else's?

Take a few moments to think about the last time you cried. Do you judge yourself for it? Now visualize what was happening in that moment, and briefly describe what emotions came up for you. Can you recall any specific thoughts that preceded those emotions?

If your life was turned into a movie, what would the description of the movie be? Who would you want to depict you and the people in your life, and why?

_____

_____

_____

_____

_____

_____

_____

_____

_____

_____

_____

_____

_____

_____

_____

_____

_____

_____

_____

_____

CORE VALUES

To find your core values, check eight words from the following list that are most important to you.

Use the blank spaces to add any values.

Truth	Flexibility	Freedom	Curiosity
Friendship	Efficiency	Commitment	Recognition
Justice	Honesty	Prosperity	Discipline
Fairness	Respect	Honor	Spirituality
Stability	Success	Self-control	Strength
Creativity	Peace	Family	Growth
Collaboration	Empathy	Harmony	Legacy
Happiness	Power	Control	Communication
Prestige	Fun	Love	Loyalty
Health	Independence	Service	Sincerity
Risk-taking	Relationships	Dependability	Beauty
Equality	Humor	Collaboration	Honor
Purpose	Wisdom	Obedience	Patience
Productivity	Adventure	Courage	Integrity
Competition	Intelligence	Hard work	Influence
Security	Trust	Community	Fulfillment
_____	_____	_____	_____
_____	_____	_____	_____

Continued >>

Look at the eight core values you chose, and narrow them down to five priorities. Rank those five values in order of importance, so that if two values ever conflict, you can make a decision between them.

1. _____

2. _____

3. _____

4. _____

5. _____

Now that you have prioritized your values, define what they mean to you, their importance, and behaviors that align with them. Using this format, try for yourself on the next page.

VALUE	DEFINITION	WHY IT'S IMPORTANT	BEHAVIORS
Example: Relationships	*Cherishing quality time with people who are important to me.*	*So that I am able to give and receive comfort and companionship.*	*Scheduling time to hang out with loved ones.* *Texting a friend when they cross my mind.*

VALUE	DEFINITION	WHY IT'S IMPORTANT	BEHAVIORS

Continued >>

What realizations did you have after doing this practice?

_____

_____

_____

_____

_____

_____

_____

_____

_____

_____

_____

_____

_____

_____

_____

_____

_____

_____

_____

_____

_____

_____

_____

Look at the core values you chose in the self-assessment. Do you see any gaps between them and your behavior? How can you go about addressing the gaps between what you believe and what you do?

Many times, core values stem from the values that were instilled in us as children by caregivers. As you look at the values you chose earlier, which ones do you value because of the people who raised you, and which come from your own experiences?

SETTING SMART GOALS

Goals are informed by values. You've ranked your top five values in order of importance. Now choose your top three values and create goals that align with them, using the SMART acronym: Specific, Measurable, Attainable, Realistic, and Timely. Do these behaviors feel reasonable or realistic for your lifestyle? What is the time span you are giving yourself to complete the goal?

Value: _____

Specific: _____

Measurable: _____

Attainable: _____

Realistic: _____

Timely: _____

Value: _____

Specific: _____

Measurable: _____

Attainable: _____

Realistic: _____

Timely: _____

Continued >>

Value: _____

Specific goal: _____

Measurable: _____

Attainable: _____

Realistic: _____

Timely: _____

What did you enjoy and/or find challenging about this practice?

_____

_____

_____

_____

_____

_____

_____

_____

_____

_____

_____

_____

_____

Write down any barriers stemming from your own beliefs. Brainstorm ways to overcome these obstacles, and hold yourself accountable. Be honest with yourself.

I am intentional
with my thoughts and
actions so that they
reflect what I value.

A huge part of CBT is reframing negative thoughts and emotions to focus on positive ones. What environments or people are bringing you joy? What have you been feeling grateful for?

BELLY BREATHING

Belly breathing is a simple exercise to help you slow your breathing and feel it in your body. Use this any time you need to relax or relieve some stress.

1. Sit or lie down in a comfortable position.

2. Place one hand on your stomach and the other hand over your heart.

3. Close your eyes if that feels more comfortable to you.

4. Take a slow, deep breath in through your nose. While doing so, let your stomach expand to push your hand out.

5. Breathe out through your mouth and let your stomach slowly collapse so that your hand comes back down.

6. Repeat this process 10 more times, and take your time with each breath.

How are you feeling after this exercise?

_____

_____

_____

_____

_____

_____

_____

_____

CHECK IN

Think back to your response to the first check-in and the problems you were experiencing. Have your thoughts and behaviors shifted to more positive ones? In what areas would you like to see improvement?

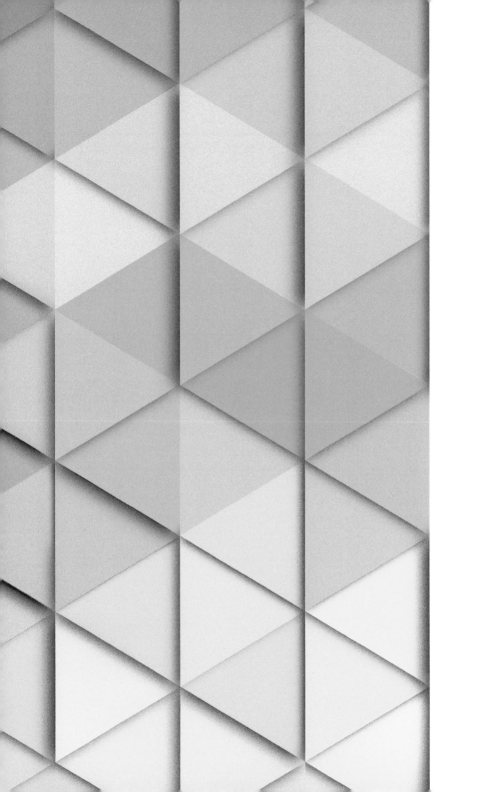

2

LOOKING INWARD

This section will help you begin the journey inward. You will use CBT principles to look within and identify your own ways of thinking, explore the negative beliefs and stories you tell yourself, and find ways to break those patterns. Your thoughts can influence your confidence, body image, and how you speak to yourself. But once you are able to pinpoint your unhelpful beliefs, you then have the ability and power to reframe or replace them with thoughts that are more beneficial and sustainable for your psychological well-being. Through the techniques and work you do in this part, you will be able to create thoughts that better reflect your current reality, instead of the *what-if*s and *should*s you may be focusing on right now.

I deserve love, respect, and peace, even when my mind tries to convince me otherwise.

CHECK IN

As you begin to explore your inner thoughts, you may realize it's not always easy to understand where these thoughts come from. What have you learned about your thought process so far? What would you like to change about it?

Take some time to think about your past week. What has been causing you the most stress or anxiety? Are you able to notice what your triggers are? What are some thoughts you can tell yourself when these triggers occur that would make you feel better?

_____

_____

_____

_____

_____

_____

_____

_____

_____

_____

_____

_____

_____

_____

_____

_____

_____

_____

_____

DEPRESSION SYMPTOM CHECKLIST

In the past month, have you persistently experienced:

☐ Little interest or pleasure in doing things

☐ Trouble sleeping

☐ Changes in appetite

☐ Feeling depressed or hopeless

☐ Feeling more tired or having lower energy than you typically would

☐ Feeling like you're a failure

☐ More trouble than usual concentrating

☐ Feeling the world would be better without you in it*

If you checked three or more boxes, you may be experiencing depression. You can learn more by talking to a mental health professional or going to the website of the National Alliance on Mental Illness (NAMI.org) for more information.

> *** If you checked this box, please put this book down and call the National Suicide Prevention Lifeline at 1-800-273-8255.**

ANXIETY SYMPTOM CHECKLIST

In the past month, have you persistently experienced:

☐ Feeling nervous, anxious, or on edge

☐ Inability to control your worries

☐ Feeling restless

☐ Difficulty relaxing

☐ Worrying about a lot of different things at once

☐ Feeling easily irritated

☐ Being afraid that something bad will happen

If you checked three or more boxes, you may be experiencing Generalized Anxiety Disorder (GAD). You can learn more by talking to a licensed mental health professional or referring to the NAMI website for more information.

How difficult have these problems made it for you to function in your daily life?

_____

_____

_____

_____

_____

_____

_____

_____

_____

NAMI states that anxiety disorders are currently the most common mental health concern in the US. It's common for someone with anxiety to also experience depression, and vice versa. Based on your responses to the self-assessments, do you think you're depressed and/or anxious? Why or why not?

BOX BREATHING

Our thoughts can make us anxious. It's helpful to slow down and find ways to self-regulate. Box breathing is a technique that can help you do so. Start by getting comfortable, and feel free to close your eyes.

1. Take a deep breath in through your nose, while counting to four.

2. Hold your breath and count to four, if you can.

3. Slowly breathe out through your mouth for four seconds.

4. Then pause for another four seconds before inhaling again.

5. Repeat these steps until you feel calm.

As a bonus, use your index finger to trace the lines of a box on your opposite palm for each step in the list.

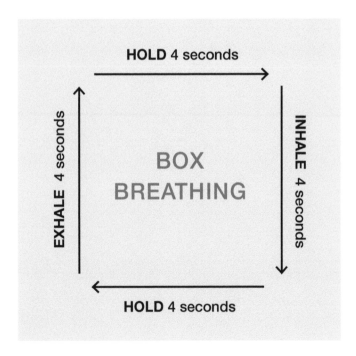

Think of your past week and the positive moments you have experienced. What about those experiences made them positive? What thoughts and emotions do you recall having at those times?

Think about how you perceive yourself (i.e., your appearance, personality, behaviors). Keep these thoughts in mind as you proceed to the next practice. What do you love about yourself? What do you wish you could change? Which question was easier to answer, and why?

The more confidence you have in yourself, the easier it can be to trust in your capabilities and make decisions that are best for you. How confident do you feel in yourself right now? How do you sometimes sabotage your self-confidence? What helps you feel your most confident?

FINDING THE EXCEPTIONS
IN OUR NEGATIVE BELIEFS

The negative thoughts we have about ourselves often stem from earlier messages we received from others. Although it's helpful to recognize where these negative thoughts come from, the true purpose of this exercise is to demonstrate that the negative thoughts aren't true, by answering the following:

WHAT ARE MY NEGATIVE BELIEFS ABOUT MYSELF?	WHERE (SPECIFIC PEOPLE OR EXPERIENCES) DID I GET THIS BELIEF FROM?	WHAT REMINDS ME THAT THIS IS NOT TRUE?
I am unloved.	I was often alone and felt ignored as a kid.	I currently have people in my life who check in on me and make me feel loved.

Write the items from the third column on sticky notes to use as personal affirmations that match your lived experiences. After doing this exercise, how are you feeling?

What I focus on
becomes my reality.
I can create the life aligned
with my values.

It's easier to treat others with compassion than ourselves. Think of any mistakes that you've made for which you haven't forgiven yourself. What is keeping you from giving yourself grace? Would you tell a friend the same things you're telling yourself?

JUST BECAUSE . . . DOESN'T MEAN

We sometimes believe our negative thoughts are factual, especially if we have examples to prove them. The first column has examples of statements that may sound valid but are actually negative self-talk. Reflect on the negative statements you make that seem true, based on your past experiences.

EXAMPLES:	YOUR NEGATIVE BELIEF THAT FEELS FACTUAL
"I'm a bad person."	
"I'm a failure."	
"I won't be successful."	

For each belief you wrote down, think of past experiences you use to validate these negative thoughts. Practice reframing these thoughts by using this template: **Just because** *(insert past experience)* **doesn't mean** *(insert the negative belief that feels factual)*. Then choose a more positive belief about yourself to add.

Example: *Just because I made a mistake doesn't mean I'm a bad person. Any mistake I make can become a lesson learned.*

_____

_____

_____

_____

_____

CHARACTERISTICS OF
FACTS AND OPINIONS

Write down three thoughts that have been bothering you lately and, using the characteristics that follow, practice determining if each thought is a fact or opinion.

Facts are:
Verifiable
Unquestionable
True
Objective
Unchangeable

Opinions are:
Not verifiable
Open for disagreement
Beliefs
Subjective
Dependent on the individual

For example.
Thought: I'm not good enough.

Is this thought verifiable? *No.*

Is this thought open for disagreement? *Yes, because everyone's definition of enough is different.*

Is this thought truth or just my belief? *This is my belief because others may see me differently.*

Is this thought objective? *No, because being enough is a subjective idea.*

Is this thought unchangeable? *No, because it can shift depending on how I feel about myself or what I'm doing.*

Thought 1: _____

_____

Is this thought a fact or an opinion, and why?

_____

_____

_____

Thought 2: _____

_____

Is this thought a fact or an opinion, and why?

_____

_____

_____

Thought 3: _____

_____

Is this thought a fact or an opinion, and why?

_____

_____

_____

Do you find that your thoughts have been rooted in fact or opinion? Can you apply this to challenge any negative thoughts that come up in the future?

_____

_____

_____

_____

_____

_____

_____

_____

_____

_____

_____

_____

_____

_____

_____

_____

_____

_____

_____

We'll cover common cognitive distortions in the next practice. For now, think of a negative thought you've had recently and ask yourself these questions: How true is this thought? What alternative thought can I replace it with?

I give myself permission
to worry less about
the future and focus
more on the present.

COMMON COGNITIVE DISTORTIONS

Cognitive distortions are automatic thoughts that can influence our emotions. Automatic thoughts occur instantly and without conscious effort. Consider which of these cognitive distortions feel familiar. Rank them from 1 to 5, with 1 being most frequent. Use this exercise to help you practice putting a name to these thoughts to call out your distorted thinking in the future.

	Magnifying or Minimizing: Overemphasizing mistakes or down-playing accomplishments.
	Catastrophizing: Only seeing the worst possible outcomes of a situation.
	Overgeneralizing: Making sweeping assumptions based on one or a few incidents.
	Personalizing: Taking responsibility for events or situations that are not your responsibility.
	Jumping to Conclusions: Assuming the meaning of a situation with little or no evidence.

What triggers lead you to have these automatic thoughts?

_____

_____

_____

_____

_____

_____

One common cognitive distortion entails discounting the positives, which means believing that your accomplishments or positive qualities don't hold as much weight as the negatives. Take some time to list what you appreciate about yourself and the accomplishments that you are proud of.

Another cognitive distortion is personalization, where you blame yourself for situations that are not your responsibility. Is this a trap that you fall into often? How can you begin to let go of some of the unnecessary burdens that you've placed on yourself?

Instead of focusing
on where I should be,
I can focus on the beauty
of where I am now.

EXAMPLES OF CORE BELIEFS

Our core beliefs are fundamental ideas about how the world works that influence how we interpret our experiences. We behave and think in accordance with our core beliefs. And because CBT is grounded in an exploration of reasons behind our thoughts and behaviors, we should practice identifying them. Using the list that follows, consider and reflect on which of these core beliefs you hold.

☐ The world is evil.

☐ There's something wrong with me.

☐ I can do whatever I put my mind to.

☐ I am safe.

☐ Nothing lasts forever.

☐ I deserve good things in life.

☐ I can't trust anyone except myself.

☐ I am unlovable.

☐ Nice people finish last.

☐ People can change.

☐ Things can always get better.

☐ I can't do anything right.

☐ If I work hard, I will succeed.

☐ Each experience is a lesson.

☐ I can count on people.

Continued >>

What emotions did this practice bring up for you? What are you noticing about yourself?

_____

_____

_____

_____

_____

_____

_____

_____

_____

_____

_____

_____

_____

_____

_____

_____

_____

_____

Are there any past experiences that you are holding on to that make it difficult to be present? What do you feel that you would need to let these events go? (i.e., an apology, a conversation) How can you give yourself what you're needing?

IDENTIFYING YOUR CORE BELIEFS

In the last practice, we focused on examples of core beliefs. Now think of your own, either negative or positive.

For example:
I am ... worthy of love.
Other people are ... trustworthy.
The world is ... dangerous.
The future is ... hopeful.

I am ... _____

_____

_____

Other people are ... _____

_____

_____

The world is ... _____

_____

_____

The future is ... _____

_____

_____

As you look at your responses, do you tend to have more negative or positive core beliefs? Why?

Review the core beliefs from the previous practice. Where do these beliefs come from? Do you feel your core beliefs accurately represent who you are? Would you like to let go of any of them?

\
\
\
\
\
\
\
\
\
\
\
\
\
\
\
\
\
\

Think about the people in your life and the messages you have received from them. Write a description of the person people expect you to be. Then write about who your authentic self is. How are these two descriptions alike, and how are they different?

DON'T *SHOULD* YOURSELF

Social media has made it easier than ever to compare yourself to others, leading you to *should* yourself. There is nothing wrong with having goals and standards for yourself. But sometimes these expectations are not realistic, are heavy to carry, and make room for disappointment and burnout. Uncover specific ways that you *should* yourself by completing the following sentences.

I should be . . . _____

_____

_____

I should not . . . _____

_____

_____

I should have . . . _____

_____

_____

I should want . . . _____

_____

_____

Take a look at what you've written, and the expectations you have of yourself. Which ones are helpful, and which are not?

_____

_____

_____

_____

_____

_____

_____

_____

_____

_____

_____

_____

_____

_____

_____

_____

_____

_____

_____

Look at your list of *should*s. Do all of them feel fair and realistic to place on yourself? Are there any *should*s that you believe because other people expect you to? How can you release the overwhelming and unfair expectations that others have placed on you?

_____

_____

_____

_____

_____

_____

_____

_____

_____

_____

_____

_____

_____

_____

_____

_____

Sometimes the negative thoughts we have can keep us stag-
nant, because of either a fear of the unknown or a desire to stay
in our comfort zone. How are your limiting beliefs holding you
back from growth opportunities? What can you tell yourself for
motivation?

IF . . . THEN . . . STATEMENTS

A common pattern of thinking is worrying about how we will be perceived. Exploring a series of *if . . . then . . .* statements can help you recognize what underlies that thought process. Think of three things you have been worrying about lately, and practice identifying this way of thinking.

For example: **If** *I say no,* **then** *I will let someone down,* **then** *they won't like me anymore,* **then** *they will leave me.*

1. If (your worry)

_____

_____

Then (what you fear will happen)

_____

_____

Then (if that happens, then what does that mean for you)

_____

_____

Then (what else does this mean for you)

_____

_____

2. If _____

_____

Then _____

_____

Then _____

_____

Then _____

_____

3. If _____

_____

Then _____

_____

Then _____

_____

Then _____

_____

What have you noticed from practicing *if . . . then* statements? Was this practice difficult for you to do?

Worry occurs when we anticipate negative events and how we will (or will not) handle them. What do you worry about the most? When you think of these concerns, what is the worst that could happen? How likely are these situations to occur?

Overcoming our fears can give us the confidence to face other challenges. Think of the last time you faced one of your fears and it lessened. Write about it here and focus on what helped you overcome that fear and how you felt when you conquered it.

There is a difference
between what I
experience and how
I choose to interpret it.

Imagine waking up and having your perfect day. Write down how you would spend it, how you would be feeling, and the thoughts you would be having. What about this day would make it perfect for you? How can you incorporate some of these things into your daily routine?

CHECK IN

With hope, this part has helped shed light on your negative beliefs. What do you think you've discovered about yourself so far? What improvements do you notice in how you think about yourself?

_____

_____

_____

_____

_____

_____

_____

_____

_____

_____

_____

_____

_____

_____

_____

_____

_____

_____

_____

_____

_____

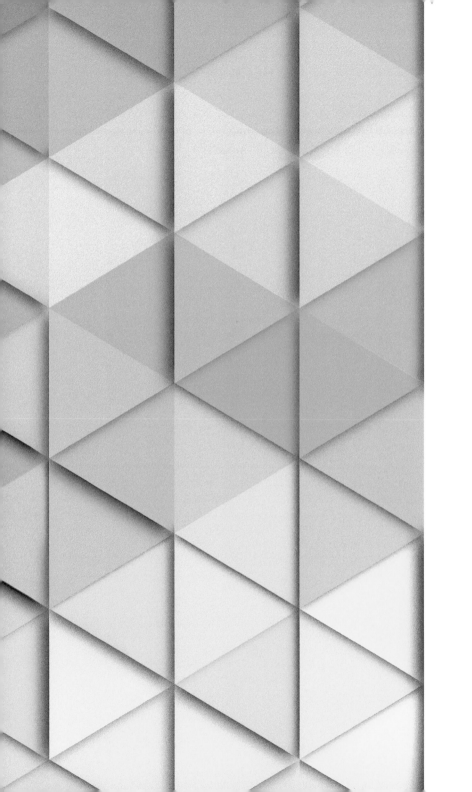

3

ADVANCING OUTWARD

As a couples and family therapist, I see firsthand how thoughts influence behaviors and relationships with others. Many of my clients struggle with feeling like they don't have enough time in the day to complete their tasks. At the same time, they are trying to navigate their boundaries with loved ones, overcome their fears, and reach their goals. Does any of this sound like you?

One of the key components of CBT is identifying and tracking patterns of behavior that are not sustainable and changing them to behaviors that work better. These patterns can look like procrastination, an imbalance between work and social time, or self-isolation. The goal of this part of the journal is to help you identify these patterns, focus on activities that bring meaning and enjoyment to your life, better manage your time, and overall improve your social well-being and relationships with others, to the best of your abilities. After all, numerous studies have shown that being involved in social relationships benefits mental and physical health. By the end of this section, my hope is that you are able to improve your healthy habits and reach out to loved ones for support.

I have the power
to choose how to
respond rather than
react unconsciously.

When you think about the important relationships in your life, who comes to mind? Have you been able to pour as much effort into those relationships as you would like? If so, how? If not, what has gotten in the way?

ALTERNATE NOSTRIL BREATHING

In a 2013 study, Anant Narayan Sinha and colleagues found that practicing alternate nostril breathing slows the heart and breathing rates and lowers blood pressure.

1. Put your index and middle fingers of your right hand on your forehead.

2. Place your thumb on your right nostril, and your ring finger on your left.

3. Close your right nostril with your thumb and inhale through your left.

4. Press on your left nostril and release your right nostril to exhale.

5. Inhale through your right nostril (while your left is closed), then exhale through your left.

6. Repeat six times.

Was this practice helpful? How are you feeling now?

_____

_____

_____

_____

_____

_____

_____

_____

Reflect on the past two weeks and how your days have been going. Are you happy with how you have spent your time? What has helped you balance your time? Are there action steps you can take to manage your time better?

MORNING AND NIGHTTIME ROUTINES

Place a check mark next to the activities that you already have as part of your morning and/or nighttime routine. Keep in mind that not all the activities listed will resonate with you as an individual. Circle the activities that you would like to incorporate more often, based on your unique values and abilities.

☐ Waking up or going to bed at the same time

☐ Reading

☐ Meditating

☐ Stretching

☐ Showering

☐ Drinking coffee/tea

☐ Reciting affirmations

☐ Eating a healthy breakfast

☐ Planning ahead for the day

☐ Listening to music

☐ Staying off social media

☐ Listening to a podcast

☐ Journaling

☐ Exercising

☐ Praying

☐ Practicing gratitude

☐ Drinking water

☐ Spending time with loved ones

How do you think adding some of these activities to your day would help your mental health?

_____

_____

_____

_____

_____

Make a list of all the obligations and responsibilities you have to take care of right now. Are you overwhelmed when you look at this list? What actions can you take to lighten your load?

When you think of how you manage your time, do you notice any tasks that you tend to put off? If so, what emotions or thoughts lead you to procrastinate? How do you feel once you notice you are procrastinating? What would help you not procrastinate?

_____

_____

_____

_____

_____

_____

_____

_____

_____

_____

_____

_____

_____

_____

_____

_____

_____

_____

I will not allow my
circumstances to eclipse
the beauty that
comes with growth.

COGNITIVE DISTORTIONS LEADING TO BEHAVIORS

Refer back to the list of cognitive distortions discussed in the last section (page 45). Reflect on how these cognitive distortions have influenced your behaviors. For each one, can you recall a time when you had one of these types of distorted automatic thoughts and what your resulting behavior was?

For example: Jumping to conclusions.

I got to work and noticed my coworker had an attitude. I automatically assumed they were mad at me or I did something wrong, so I avoided them for the rest of the day.

Magnifying or Minimizing:

Catastrophizing:

Overgeneralizing:

Personalizing:

Jumping to Conclusions:

Now that you're aware of cognitive distortions and their influence on your behaviors, how will you be more mindful of this in the future?

Uncertainty can make us uneasy because we like to know what to expect. When was the last time you felt uncertain about how something would turn out? What emotions came up for you? How did you handle them?

BEHAVIORS YOU'D LIKE TO CHANGE

This section identifies behavior patterns and what drives them. Following is a list of common behaviors that generally aren't healthy. Check off any behaviors that you find yourself doing.

☐ Isolating from loved ones

☐ Procrastinating

☐ Yelling at others

☐ Crying often

☐ Ghosting people

☐ Using drugs/alcohol to escape

☐ Finding it difficult to start your day

☐ Criticizing yourself

☐ Frequently complaining

☐ Not eating enough

☐ Overeating

☐ Throwing objects out of anger

☐ Blaming others

Of the behaviors that you checked off, which ones would you like to change or improve? Keep these behaviors in mind to use in the next practice.

_____

_____

_____

_____

_____

_____

PROS AND CONS OF BEHAVIOR

Look at Behaviors You'd Like to Change (page 81) and take some action. Choose the behavior you would like to change the most, and write it here.

Example: Isolating from others

Behavior: _____

_____

Consider the pros (positive impacts) and the cons (negative impacts). Rank the importance of each pro and con to you on a scale of 1 to 5, with 1 being not important at all.

PROS OF BEHAVIOR	IMPORTANCE
Example: I get alone time.	*4*
Total:	

CONS OF BEHAVIOR	IMPORTANCE
Example: I push away people who care about me.	*5*
Total:	

Do the costs (cons) of this behavior outweigh the benefits (pros)? If so, is there an alternative behavior? If not, or if there's a tie, reflect on why this is still a behavior that you want to change.

What activities do you engage in that bring joy to your day or life? What activities do you engage in that feel draining? Do you find yourself doing more energizing or draining activities? How can you prioritize more joyful activities in your life?

LEARNING YOUR ABCS

Rational Emotive Behavioral Therapy (REBT) is a form of CBT. A core concept of REBT is the ABC model, which shows how your belief about an event affects your behaviors and emotions. To bring this out of the realm of theory, use the chart to think about three actual recent situations (positive or negative) and how they affected your beliefs and behaviors:

A—ACTIVATING EVENT	B—BELIEFS	C—CONSEQUENCES
What situation occurred?	**What automatic thoughts did I have? What beliefs about myself came to mind?**	**As a reaction, how did I behave? What emotions/physical sensations came up for me?**
Example: I slept through my alarm and woke up late.	*Example: I'm a lazy and late person. My whole day is ruined.*	*Example: I felt disappointed in myself and stayed in bed even longer.*

What do you recognize about yourself after the "Learning your ABCs" practice?

EXPANDING THE ABCS

Using the activating events from the last exercise, practice expanding on your ABCs by disputing the belief and creating new beliefs and behaviors.

Activating Event

For example: I slept through my alarm and woke up late.

Beliefs

For example: I'm a lazy and late person. My whole day is ruined.

Consequences

For example: I felt disappointed in myself and stayed in bed even longer.

Dispute the Beliefs

For example: Maybe sleeping through the alarm was my body showing me I need more rest.

Continued >>

Effective New Beliefs/Behaviors

For example: I'm not a lazy person for needing more rest. I can try going to sleep earlier.

_____

_____

What did you find helpful about this practice? How can you implement it in your daily life?

_____

_____

_____

_____

_____

_____

_____

_____

_____

_____

_____

*"Loneliness expresses the pain of being alone.
Solitude expresses the glory of being alone."*

–PAUL TILLICH

When do you find yourself feeling lonely? When do you find yourself enjoying your solitude? What would you say is the difference between these two experiences? How can you enjoy your alone time more?

_____

_____

_____

_____

_____

_____

_____

_____

_____

_____

_____

_____

_____

_____

_____

BREAKING UP GOALS INTO ACTIONABLE STEPS AND REWARDS

In part 1, you developed SMART goals based on your values (page 15). Revisit that exercise, choose one of your SMART goals, and now apply it to your life:

Example SMART Goal: To not yell or lash out at loved ones when distressed.

SMART Goal: _____

Think of a task that would help you achieve this goal, and three steps needed to fulfill this task.

Example: Communicate my emotions calmly.

1. *Practice breathing exercises to calm down.*

2. *Journal my emotions out first.*

3. *Express myself using I statements (see Communicating Effectively, page 96).*

Task: _____

Steps:

1. _____

2. _____

3. _____

Now decide how you will reward yourself for completing each step so that you have something to look forward to.

Example: Express how proud you are of yourself, or do something fun with a loved one.

Rewards:

1. _____

2. _____

3. _____

Did you find this exercise helpful? How do you think connecting a reward to your tasks will help you achieve your goals?

_____

_____

_____

_____

_____

_____

_____

_____

_____

_____

_____

_____

I don't have to handle
everything on my own.
I have people who love
and care for me.

REWARD YOURSELF

Rewards are often used as motivation to stay consistent with habits and goals we want to accomplish. When a desirable outcome follows behavior, that behavior is more likely to continue. Create a list of activities that you find rewarding. Next to each activity, write how often you'd like to do that activity.

Here are a few tips:

1. They must be desirable. They have to feel beneficial to you.

2. They shouldn't negate what you just achieved. For instance, if you're rewarding yourself for working out, it may be helpful to have a non-food-related reward.

3. They should be given consistently, to provide motivation.

How was this activity for you? Was it difficult to come up with rewards for yourself?

Consider the expression "Birds of a feather flock together." Do you agree with this? Think of the three people you spend the most time with. What behaviors and/or goals do you have that are similar to theirs? Do they motivate you to achieve the goals you set for yourself?

Examine the relationships you have in your life. Are you happy with these relationships? Do you notice any behaviors of yours that affect your relationships in negative and/or positive ways? What changes in behavior can you make to improve the relationships?

COMMUNICATING EFFECTIVELY

One essential aspect of healthy relationships is communication. Here are a few rules to help you practice more effective communication:

1. Use *I* statements to take ownership of your emotions instead of blaming.

2. Focus on one problem at a time instead of listing multiple complaints.

3. Express a request instead of a demand.

For example:
I feel *neglected and alone* **when** *we don't spend quality time together.*
I would appreciate it if *we planned at least two date nights a month.*

Think of the last time someone hurt your feelings, and use the following template to express yourself.

I felt _____
(Your emotions)

when _____.
(Describe the problem objectively)

I would appreciate it if _____

_____.
(Make a request instead of demanding change)

How do you think your conversations with others would go if you used this template to express yourself?

_____

_____

_____

_____

_____

_____

_____

_____

_____

_____

_____

_____

_____

_____

_____

_____

_____

_____

Nedra Glover Tawwab, a fellow therapist and relationship expert, defines boundaries as expectations and needs that help us feel safe and comfortable within our relationships. Who do you have difficulties setting boundaries with in your life? Why is it difficult?

Sometimes your social life can cause a great deal of anxiety, especially if you are worried about how others may perceive you and your actions. When you think about your social circle, is there anyone who makes you feel judged? Who do you feel safe to be yourself around?

I will shift my focus
to improving what I have
instead of always feeling
pressured to do something new.

DON'T *SHOULD* OTHERS, EITHER

The Don't *Should* Yourself practice (page 56) discussed how the expectations you put on yourself are not always realistic and can make room for disappointment. The same can happen in relationships, especially if these *should*s are unspoken or assumed. Explore how you *should* others by thinking of one person you have expectations of (a partner, child, coworker).

For example:

A person I have expectations of: my mom.
She should be loving and forgiving at all times.
She should always answer me when I call.
She should want to spend as much time as she can with me.

A person I have expectations of: _____

They should be . . .

_____

_____

_____

They should _____ me . . .

_____

_____

They should want to _____ with me . . .

_____

_____

Take a look at the expectations you set on the previous page. Which ones are healthy standards of how you should be treated? Which might be rooted in comparison or may be unreasonable?

_____

_____

_____

_____

_____

_____

_____

_____

_____

_____

_____

_____

_____

_____

_____

_____

_____

_____

_____

Who in your life makes you feel drained after spending time with them? How and why? Why do you think you continue to spend time with them, and are there boundaries you can establish to protect your energy?

Who do you reach out for when you're experiencing feelings of loneliness? Does this person make you feel energized and cared for after spending time with them? What about this person or the time spent with them is rewarding for you? Do you find that you prioritize spending time with them?

Embracing uncertainty can be more beneficial than worrying because you accept that you don't know everything. Has needing certainty in life been helpful or unhelpful to you? Do you tend to predict that something bad will happen just because you're uncertain?

The older we get, the harder it can be to maintain long-lasting friendships, leading us to feel isolated or lonely. Among work, families, and "me" time, it can be hard to nurture friendships. Are there any friendships that you would like to pour more effort into? How can you do so?

RELATIONSHIP GOALS

To improve your social well-being, it's helpful to set goals. When we've talked about goals so far, it has been focused on personal values and achievements or has been geared toward how to formulate them. For this practice, create goals for the social aspects of your life. For each category, write one goal for improvement, using the SMART goals format. If there is an area that doesn't apply to you (i.e., no romantic partner or child), feel free to replace it with another relationship.

Relationship with a family member

_____

_____

_____

Relationship with a friend

_____

_____

_____

Relationship with a coworker

_____

_____

_____

Relationship with a romantic partner

_____

_____

_____

Relationship with a child

_____

_____

_____

Have you ever set goals for your social relationships before? How was this practice for you?

_____

_____

_____

_____

_____

_____

_____

_____

_____

What are important qualities that you look for in a friend?
What are important qualities you look for in a romantic partner?
Do you feel as though you bring these same qualities to
your relationships?

When was the last time you asked someone for help? Who was it, and what did you need help with? Do you find it difficult to ask others for help, and in what situations? Why or why not?

_____

_____

_____

_____

_____

_____

_____

_____

_____

_____

_____

_____

_____

_____

_____

_____

_____

_____

_____

I am capable of
finding a solution
to my problems.

When was the last time you volunteered or did something to serve your community? How did it make you feel to help others in need? Would you like to incorporate more volunteer opportunities into your schedule?

CHECK IN

Since starting this book, I have been able to:

- ☐ Ask someone for help
- ☐ Volunteer
- ☐ Work toward a goal
- ☐ Spend time with someone I love
- ☐ Manage my time better
- ☐ Do an activity I enjoy

What areas in your life do you feel still have room for improvement?

_____

_____

_____

_____

_____

_____

_____

_____

_____

_____

_____

_____

_____

_____

_____

_____

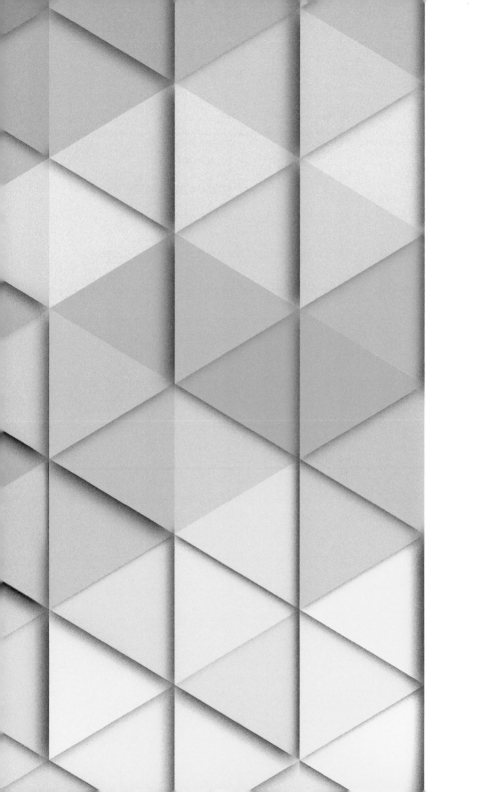

4

MOVING FORWARD

So far, you've gained insight into your thought processes, behavioral patterns, and how you can alter the negative ones to improve the psychological and social aspects of your mental health. The last component of CBT is how thoughts and behaviors affect emotions. This is important because how you handle your emotions is a major determinant in your mental health.

How you choose to perceive a situation determines how you feel about it. For instance, graduations symbolize the end of one part and the beginning of a new one, simultaneously. One person may be entrenched in the negative or sad feelings that come with their journey ending. Another person may feel excitement about the new beginning. This section provides you with techniques to help you shift your perceptions and manage difficult emotions when they arise.

I can't always change
what's happening around me,
but I can change
what happens within me.

CHECK IN

Think about the emotions that you have been experiencing lately. Have they been more positive or negative? Would you like to improve the way you handle your emotions? How so?

_____

_____

_____

_____

_____

_____

_____

_____

_____

_____

_____

_____

_____

_____

_____

_____

_____

SAFE PLACE

This practice is used in Eye Movement Desensitization and Reprocessing (EMDR) therapy to help clients create a safe space for processing trauma. The purpose here is for you to create a place to go in your mind when you're experiencing distressing emotions.

Think of a place, real or imaginary, that makes you feel at peace. As you visualize yourself there, what do you notice with your senses? How does your body feel? What word best describes this space? Practice returning to your peaceful place, especially when you feel annoyed. Write down what you notice and if it's been helpful.

Think of how you were feeling before you began using this journal. What emotions had you been experiencing that led you to pick up this book? Now think of how you're feeling in this present moment. Do you notice any changes in your emotions since you've been using this journal?

Consider what emotions you feel throughout a typical day. As you reflect on your usual routine, during what part of your day do you feel the best? Why do you think that is?

SELF-CARE ASSESSMENT

Think of three ways that you take care of yourself in the categories that follow. If you are unable to think of three, note how you would like to take care of yourself instead.

Physical *(e.g., sleeping, exercising, eating healthy, attending doctors' appointments)*

1. _____
2. _____
3. _____

Emotional *(e.g., journaling, expressing emotions, doing something you enjoy)*

1. _____
2. _____
3. _____

Social *(e.g., spending time with loved ones, asking for help, checking in on others)*

1. _____
2. _____
3. _____

Spiritual *(e.g., praying/meditating, behaving in alignment with values)*

1. _____

2. _____

3. _____

Professional *(e.g., learning new job skills, setting boundaries at work)*

1. _____

2. _____

3. _____

Based on your responses, in what areas of your self-care are you doing well, and where could you use some improvement?

_____

_____

_____

_____

_____

_____

_____

_____

_____

_____

When was the last time you recall feeling content with your life? What was happening at that time? Do you think your self-care practices at that time contributed to how good you were feeling? How can you return to feeling more content?

Our upbringing can influence how we express and process our emotions. Reflect on your childhood and how you were raised. Which emotions did you see adults in your household express often? How did they express these emotions to others? Do you express your emotions the same way?

MOOD TRACKER

Choose five moods or emotions that you typically experience in a regular week. Then choose five colors to correspond with these moods.

MOODS	COLORS

Use the legend above to complete a mood tracker for the next two weeks. At the end of each day, color in whichever mood best described how you felt that day.

DAY	1	2	3	4	5	6	7	8	9	10	11	12	13	14
MOOD														

What does your mood tracker show you? Have you seen any improvement in your mood? What do you think has helped you improve? If not, what can you do to improve your mood?

_____

_____

_____

_____

_____

Sometimes our behaviors are rooted in our insecurities (which create the invalid thoughts that we believe about ourselves). Think back to the last time you felt insecure. What was it that made you feel that way? What would you say your insecurities are, and where do you think they are rooted?

THE PURPOSE OF EMOTIONS

I believe emotions are neither negative nor positive; rather, they are cues that we should heed. What is negative or positive (unhealthy or healthy) is our behavior in reaction to our emotions. Consider some emotions that are typically viewed in a negative light, and answer the following questions to help you practice delving into these emotions a bit further.

Emotions:

For example: Anger

1. Anger

2. Jealousy

3. Guilt

4. Sadness

5. Fear

6. _____

7. _____

What is this emotion trying to tell you?

Example: A boundary or expectation I have was violated, and I feel hurt.

1. _____

2. _____

3. _____

4. _____

5. _____

6. _____

7. _____

What do you tell yourself about this emotion when you feel it?

Example: Being angry makes me mean, and as a woman, especially a Black woman, I can't show my anger because I'll be seen as a stereotype.

1. _____
2. _____
3. _____
4. _____
5. _____
6. _____
7. _____

What is one positive aspect of feeling this emotion?

Example: It reminds me of what I feel passionate about and the boundaries that are important to me.

1. _____
2. _____
3. _____
4. _____
5. _____
6. _____
7. _____

Continued >>

What could you tell yourself instead that allows you to feel this emotion without judgment?

Example: Being angry doesn't make me mean; it reminds me that I have standards about how I deserve to be treated.

1. _____

2. _____

3. _____

4. _____

5. _____

6. _____

7. _____

What did you find helpful about this practice?

_____

_____

_____

_____

_____

_____

_____

What difficult emotions would you say you experience most often (sadness, anger, guilt, jealousy, etc.)? Do you find it difficult to accept yourself when these emotions come up for you? Why? What do you do when you notice yourself feeling this way?

Are there any decisions or moments that you regret in your life? Do you find yourself still holding on to any guilt or shame about them? Write a letter to yourself offering forgiveness and compassion.

_____

_____

_____

_____

_____

_____

_____

_____

_____

_____

_____

_____

_____

_____

_____

_____

_____

_____

_____

_____

My calm can be a powerful weapon in overcoming difficult situations.

PRACTICING GRATITUDE

Practicing gratitude is a great way to shift your attitude. Gratitude helps us operate from a place of abundance by acknowledging and focusing on what we do have and are thankful for. Answer the following questions to practice.

List three things you notice in your present surroundings that you're grateful for.

1. _____

2. _____

3. _____

Recall three moments in your life that you are grateful for experiencing.

1. _____

2. _____

3. _____

Name three people in your life that you are grateful for, and why.

1. _____

2. _____

3. _____

How do you express your gratitude for others?

_____

_____

_____

After finishing this exercise, reflect on how practicing gratitude makes
you feel.

_____

_____

_____

_____

_____

_____

_____

_____

_____

_____

_____

_____

Think of a song that matches your current mood or what you're experiencing. Play the song. As you listen, what emotions are coming up for you? What lyrics do you feel resonate with you the most? Do you want this song to represent your life? Why or why not?

CHEW IT OVER

Mindfulness is being aware of, and grounded in, the present moment and calmly accepting whatever feelings and thoughts come up. There are multiple ways to incorporate mindfulness into your daily life. One way is to pair it with activities you already do, like eating. Try it for one meal a day.

1. Start with a small item of food, and explore the food slowly before you begin to eat it.

2. Notice what it looks like, what color and texture it has.

3. Close your eyes, and focus on how the food smells and feels.

4. Put the food in your mouth and chew slowly, concentrating on its taste and your movements.

What did you enjoy about this practice? What did you find to be difficult?

_____

_____

_____

_____

_____

_____

_____

_____

_____

_____

Drawing can sometimes be more helpful than writing (or may just engage a different part of you) for tuning in to and expressing emotions you have trouble putting into words. Images sometimes create clarity that words cannot. Draw a picture of how you think other people in your life see you. Then, next to it, draw a picture of how you see yourself. What differences do you notice?

SELF-CARE BINGO

There are plenty of ways to take care of yourself. This activity can be a fun way to keep track of how you've been doing each week. In the blanks, add some of your own self-care activities.

Journaled	Spent time in nature		Listened to music	Spoke to someone I love
	Exercised	Took a nap	Set a boundary	Got some fresh air
Got 7+ hours of sleep	Meditated	**Used this journal**		Took myself out on a date
Stretched		Cleaned my home	Ate a healthy meal	Did something creative
Read a book	Watched my favorite movie	Unplugged from screens	Bought something nice for myself	

What did you notice about yourself from this practice?

Uncertainty about the future can be scary, but it can also be liberating.

5 (SELF-)LOVE LANGUAGES

Gary Chapman originally created the 5 Love Languages for couples, but then created a singles edition to help individuals understand their own needs and what resonates with them. For this practice, think of (and implement) three ways you can show yourself love in each language.

QUALITY TIME *Example: Spend time alone*	1. _____ 2. _____ 3. _____
PHYSICAL TOUCH *Example: Give myself a foot massage*	1. _____ 2. _____ 3. _____
ACTS OF SERVICE *Example: Prepare healthy meals for myself*	1. _____ 2. _____ 3. _____
WORDS OF AFFIRMATION *Example: Write down my accomplishments*	1. _____ 2. _____ 3. _____
GIFTS *Example: Buy myself flowers*	1. _____ 2. _____ 3. _____

Thinking of the exercise on the previous page, which love languages were easiest and most difficult to come up with activities for? Through which love languages would you like others to show you love?

_____

_____

_____

_____

_____

_____

_____

_____

_____

_____

_____

_____

_____

_____

_____

_____

_____

_____

_____

_____

Emotional resilience is the ability to adapt to and bounce back from stressful situations. One factor of resilience is managing emotions and impulses in a healthy way. What behaviors do you engage in to handle your stressors? Would you consider these behaviors healthy for you? Why or why not?

MIRROR, MIRROR, ON THE WALL

Self-esteem and body image are aspects of our personality that aren't always thought to contribute to our mental health, but they do. Boosting how we view and feel about ourselves can improve our emotional well-being.

Look at yourself in the mirror (or with your phone's camera). Take a deep breath, and stare at yourself for 30 seconds.

Write down what you appreciate about yourself.

_____

_____

_____

Return to your mirror, look at yourself, and say, "I love you."

What emotions came up for you as you did this practice? Was it difficult to look at your reflection and say positive things? Why or why not?

_____

_____

_____

_____

_____

_____

_____

_____

_____

To cope with distressing emotions, it's necessary to accept them instead of distracting yourself or denying them. Think of any troublesome emotions you've experienced recently. List the emotions in the space that follows, and write statements giving yourself permission to explore why you are feeling this way without any judgment.

What is your definition of compassion? How do you express compassion to others? How do you express compassion to yourself? Are there limits to how much compassion you give? Is there anything that makes it difficult for you to be compassionate toward yourself and others?

_____

_____

_____

_____

_____

_____

_____

_____

_____

_____

_____

_____

_____

_____

_____

_____

_____

_____

I am capable of
choosing healthy
coping strategies
over negative ones
I've used in the past.

YOUR MENTAL HEALTH PLAN

As you near the end of this journal, my hope is that you're able to take what you've learned so far and apply it to your life. This chart will help you practice and make a plan for when distressing moments arise.

TRIGGERS	WARNING SIGNS	COPING STRATEGIES
What brings up your distressing emotions and behaviors? (who, what, when)	**When can you tell your mental health is being challenged? (thoughts, emotions, bodily sensations, behaviors)**	**What can you do to make yourself feel better? (self-care activities, visualization, meditation, breathing exercises, mindfulness)**
Example: Hearing loud noises	*Example: My heart races and my palms get sweaty.*	*Example: I can listen to a song I like, and take deep breaths.*

Do you feel like this practice will be helpful for managing your triggers in the future? How?

_____

_____

_____

_____

_____

_____

_____

_____

_____

_____

_____

_____

_____

_____

_____

_____

_____

_____

Using creativity for self-expression can reveal our conscious and unconscious emotions. Some examples include painting, drawing, coloring, or writing poetry. Which creative outlets do you find helpful in processing your emotions? What about the activity helps you do so? Make time to do something creative this week.

CREATING YOUR OWN
SELF-CARE BOX

It's important to have resources and tools that you can take with you to sustain your self-care. You've already created a mental health plan for when distressing emotions come up. Now create a self-care box to use when you're in need of relaxation. Choose any container you like, then assemble a collection based on the suggestions below, adjusting the numbers and types of items to suit you, specifically.

- **Three items you can see** (photographs, book, affirmations)

- **Two items you can hear** (white noise machine, favorite album/playlist)

- **Three items you can feel** (face/foot masks, stress ball, soft blanket)

- **Two items you can smell** (essential oils, candles)

- **Three items you can taste** (chocolate, tea, nuts)

Look at your self-care box. How do you feel when you see the items inside of it? Was this practice useful for you? Why or why not?

I will not feel
guilty for taking time
to rest. I deserve
moments to unwind.

Has the way you manage your thoughts, behaviors, and emotions shifted since you began working in this journal? What improvements do you notice, and how do they make you feel? How will you use the skills you've learned in this book to continue moving forward?

CHECK IN

Since starting this journal, I have been able to:

☐ Practice self-care ☐ Calm myself down

☐ Practice gratitude ☐ Learn coping skills

☐ Identify my emotions ☐ Improve my self-esteem

☐ Express my emotions in a
healthy way

What changes are you proud of yourself for making?

_____

_____

_____

_____

_____

_____

_____

_____

_____

_____

_____

_____

_____

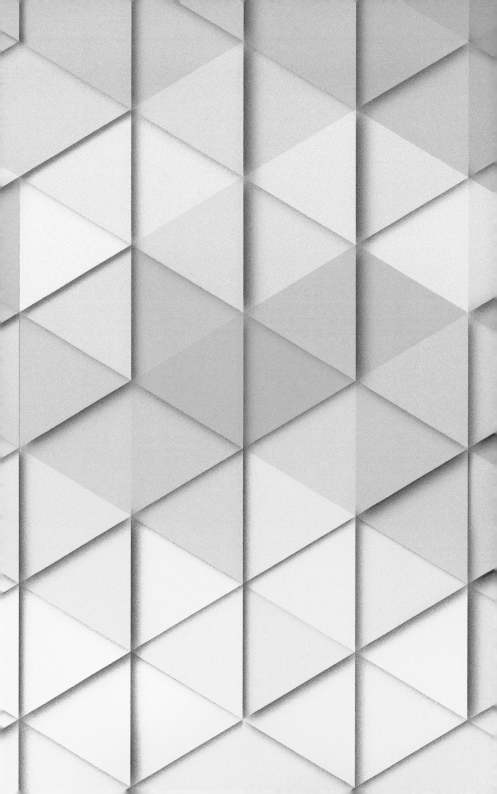

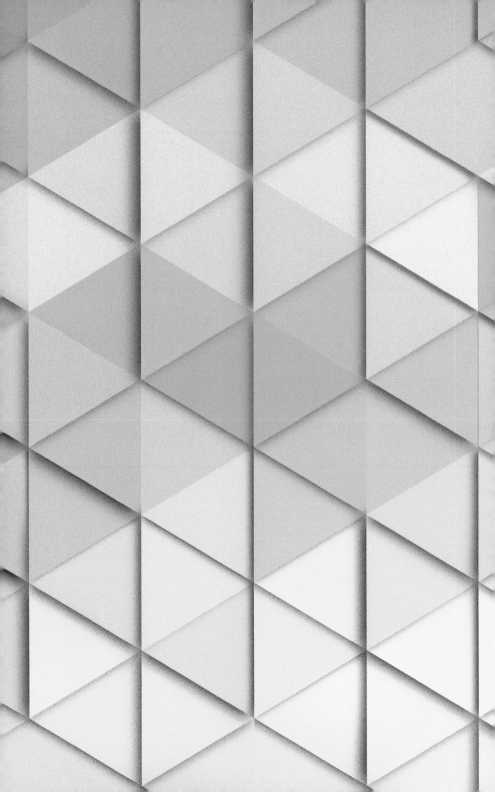

Resources

BOOKS

If you enjoyed this journal and would like to use other books as resources, here are a few you might find useful.

Set Boundaries, Find Peace, by Nedra Glover Tawwab, focuses on the importance of boundaries and how enforcing them can change your life. Each part ends with exercises and journal prompts for practice.

The Mindful Self-Compassion Workbook, by Kristin Neff and Christopher Germer, is great for learning what self-compassion is, the benefits of practicing it, and how to implement it despite difficult emotions and relationships.

After the Rain, by Alexandra Elle, provides 15 lessons on healing, self-love, and acceptance through storytelling, while also including affirmations and journal prompts for readers.

WEBSITES AND STUDIES

TherapistAid.com is a phenomenal resource for worksheets that you can use to practice skills and continue to explore your thoughts and behavior.

NAMI.org is a great website that provides information about a variety of mental health challenges, their warning signs and symptoms, fact sheets, support groups, and more.

This study provides a great overview of how effective CBT is for treating a variety of conditions, such as substance use, depression, anxiety, eating disorders, trauma, and more:

Hofmann, Stefan G. et al. (2012). "The Efficacy of Cognitive Behavioral Therapy: A Review of Meta-analyses." *Cognitive therapy and research, 36* (5), 427–440. https://doi.org/10.1007/s10608-012-9476-1

APPS

If you're looking for ways to incorporate self-care into your routine, try these apps:

Shine helps you practice gratitude and set intentions. The app also has self-help articles, meditations, and community posts to connect with others.

Ladder helps you stick to good habits. It also offers meditations, journal prompts, and mood tracking

Eternal Sunshine sends daily affirmations. They also have guided meditations and mindfulness music.

Headspace offers breathing and mindfulness exercises. It also provides focus playlists and meditations to help you wind down at night.

References

Chapman, Gary. *The 5 Love Languages: Singles Edition*. Chicago: Northfield Publishing, 2004.

Davis Bush, Ashley. *Simple Self-Care for Therapists: Restorative Practices to Weave Through Your Workday*. New York: W. W. Norton & Company, 2015.

Epstein, Norman, and Donald Baucom. *Enhanced Cognitive-Behavioral Therapy for Couples*. Washington DC: American Psychological Association, 2002.

Gehart, Diane. *Theory and Treatment Planning in Family Therapy: A Competency-Based Approach*. Boston: Cengage Learning, 2015.

Shapiro, Francine. *Eye Movement Desensitization and Reprocessing (EMDR) Therapy: Basic Principles, Protocols, and Procedures*. New York: Guilford Press, 2018.

Tillich, Paul. *The Eternal Now*. New York: Scribner, 1963.

ACKNOWLEDGMENTS

Thanks be to God for providing me with the creativity and discipline for this project. Huge thanks to Callisto Media for giving me the opportunity to create this journal, and to everyone who worked with me to bring this work to fruition. To my family and friends, thank you all so much for supporting my endeavors and always believing in me. Last, thank you to my clients and followers for being great inspiration for this work.

ABOUT THE AUTHOR

 Jordan A. Madison, LCMFT, is a licensed clinical marriage and family therapist. She is Prepare/Enrich certified, and also trained in Eye Movement Desensitization Reprocessing (EMDR) therapy. She received her BA in psychology from Spelman College, and MS in couple and family therapy from the University of Maryland. She owns and practices at Therapy Is My J.A.M., LLC, a private practice that helps individuals and couples heal from their pasts to understand their present and create the future they desire. She is passionate about reducing the stigmas around mental health and therapy, especially within the Black community. She uses her Instagram platform, @therapyismyJAM, to promote conversations and educate others on building and maintaining healthy relationships, as well as normalizing and prioritizing self-care.